Rick Hansen

Terry Barber

ACTS OF
COURAGE
SERIES

Rick Hansen is published by
Grass Roots Press, a division of Literacy Services of Canada Ltd.

PHONE 1–888–303–3213
WEBSITE www.literacyservices.com

ACKNOWLEDGMENTS

We would like to thank the Rick Hansen Foundation for supplying the majority of the photographs. For more information, visit the Rick Hansen website at www.rickhansen.com

We acknowledge the financial support of the Government of Canada through the Book Publishing Industry Development Program (BPIDP) for our publishing activities.

We acknowledge the support of
the Alberta Foundation for the Arts
for our publishing programs.

Editor: Dr. Pat Campbell
Image research: Dr. Pat Campbell and Terry Barber
Book design: Lara Minja, Lime Design Inc.

Library and Archives Canada Cataloguing in Publication

Barber, Terry, date
          Rick Hansen / Terry Barber.

ISBN 978-1-894593-82-3

          1. Hansen, Rick, 1957- 2. Athletes with disabilities—Canada—
Biography. 3. Paraplegics—Canada—Biography. 4. Readers for new
literates. I. Title.

PE1126.N43B3663 2008   428.6'2   C2008-901988-1

Printed in Canada

Contents

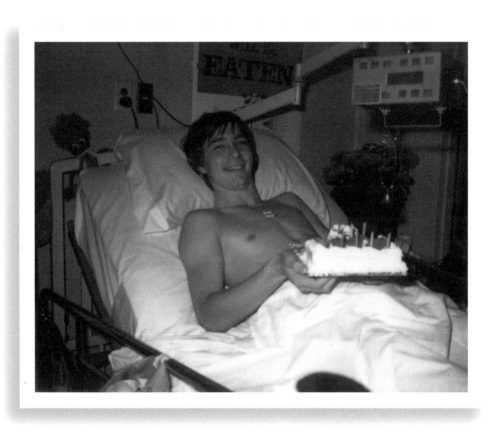

Rick smiles on his 16th birthday.

1973

Rick is in a hospital. He lies in a bed. Rick wants to get out of the bed. He wants to walk again. Rick tries to move his toes. His toes will not move. No matter how hard Rick tries, his toes will not move.

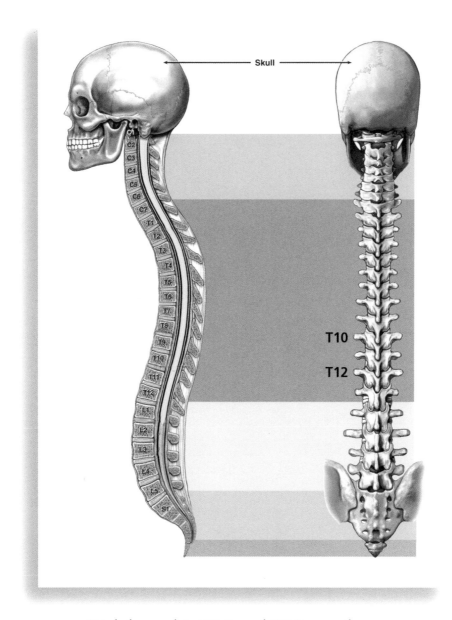

Rick hurts his T10 and T12 **vertebrae.**

1973

Rick has a spinal cord injury. Rick can move his upper body. He cannot move his lower body. Rick learns he will not walk again. He must use a wheelchair. Rick will use a wheelchair as no one ever has.

Rick and his friends love to fish.

Early Years

Rick Hansen grows up in British Columbia. He grows up in small towns. Rick has lots of energy. He loves to fish. He loves to hunt. He loves sports. Rick spends his time doing what he loves.

Rick is born on August 26, 1957.

Rick and his friends drive home.

Rick's Life Changes

Rick's life changes on June 27, 1973. He is 15 years old. Rick and two friends are driving home after a fishing trip. Their truck crashes. The boys are not hurt. They cannot drive their truck home. The truck needs to be fixed.

Hitching a ride.

Rick's Life Changes

Rick and one of his friends decide to hitchhike. They get a ride in a pickup truck. They sit in the box of the pickup truck. Rick is glad to get a ride. He wants to get home.

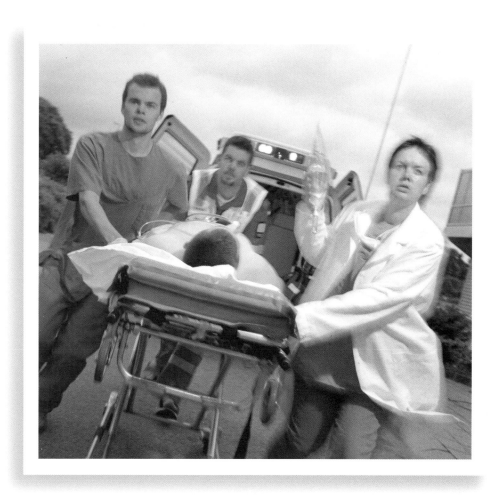

Rick's Life Changes

Rick does not make it home. Rick is in another crash. The pickup truck rolls. A large steel toolbox is tossed from the truck. Rick is tossed from the truck, too. He lands on the edge of the toolbox. Rick's back snaps. He is taken to the hospital.

Rick has hopes and dreams.

Rick's Strong Will

Rick learns he will not walk again. Rick feels sad and angry. He feels cheated. A strong **will** burns inside Rick. He wants to make the most of his life. Rick will not let his injury hold him back.

Rick gets his university degree in 1986.

Rick's Strong Will

Rick gets on with his life. Life using a wheelchair is a challenge. Rick is up for the challenge. He has goals and dreams. He finishes high school. He goes to university. Rick wants to be a gym teacher.

Rick goes to the University of British Columbia.

Rick plays table tennis.

World-Class Athlete

Rick plays sports using his wheelchair. He likes to play basketball. He likes to play volleyball. He likes to play table tennis. Rick's wheelchair becomes like a part of him. Rick becomes a world-class athlete.

In 1983, Wayne Gretzky and Rick Hansen are named outstanding athletes of the year.

Rick races in the 1982 Pan Am Games.

World-Class Athlete

It is 1979. Rick enters the world's first wheelchair marathon race. He comes in third. Rick trains harder. Over the next four years, Rick wins 19 races in a row. He is the best marathon racer in the world.

Rick competes in a wheelchair race in the 1984 Olympic Games.

The distance around the world is 40,075 km.

A New Challenge

By 1983, Rick wants a new challenge.
He wants to wheel around the world.
He wants his trip to have a purpose.
Rick wants to change society's
attitudes about people with disabilities.
He decides to wheel 40,075 km
(24,902 miles).

Rick
also wants to
raise money for
spinal cord injury
research.

Rick and his team

A New Challenge

Rick calls his trip the Man In Motion World Tour. He needs a team to help him. One person plans the trip. One person cooks the meals. One person cares for Rick's injuries. Each person has special skills.

People donate money at Expo 86.

Man In Motion World Tour

It is March 1985. The Man In Motion World Tour starts in Vancouver. Rick's team has lots of **spunk** and little money. They need money to raise money. They need to pay for hotels, food, and gas. Rick plans to raise this money on the go.

Rick wheels in China.
April 1986

Man In Motion World Tour

Rick likes to wheel 112 km (70 miles) every day. Most people would find it hard to bike 112 km. It is much harder to push a wheelchair. Pushing with your arms is much harder than using your legs.

On average, Rick wheels 8 hours every day.

Rick wheels in a storm.

Man In Motion World Tour

Imagine being Rick. You climb up a long, steep hill. A cold, strong wind blows in your face. Your upper body hurts. Your wrists feel as if they will explode. You feel awful. And you have to do the same thing the next day.

Rick wears out 160 wheelchair tires on the tour.

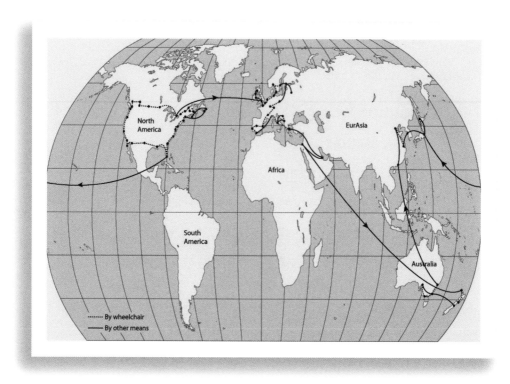

Man In Motion World Tour

Man In Motion World Tour

Day after day, Rick keeps going. Rick and his team visit 34 countries in two years. People around the world support the Man In Motion World

Tour. Rick shows the world what a person with a disability can do.

Rick wheels in Paris.

Rick starts the Canadian tour

in Cape Spear, Newfoundland.

Man In Motion World Tour

The Man In Motion World Tour is not raising much money. The tour returns to Canada in August 1986. Then, the money comes. Canadians open their wallets and hearts. The Man In Motion World Tour raises over $26 million.

It takes Rick 10 months to wheel across Canada.

Rick finishes the Man In Motion World Tour
on May 22, 1987.

Man In Motion World Tour

It is May 1987. The Man In Motion World Tour ends where it began, in Vancouver. Rick wheels the last 50 yards. Rick sees a **banner**. The top line of the banner reads, THE END IS JUST THE BEGINNING.

The banner is telling Rick what his future holds.

The Man In Motion World Tour lasts two years, two months, and two days.

Rick marries Amanda in 1987.

Man In Motion World Tour

Rick does not earn money from the tour. He gets much more. Rick falls in love with a team member. Her name is Amanda Reid. Rick marries Amanda after the tour. They have three girls.

Rick and his family, 2005

Rick Hansen

Goals and Dreams

Today, Rick works toward two goals. The first goal is to make life better for people with disabilities. The second goal is to raise money for research. One day, this research will help injured people walk again.

Goals and Dreams

Rick's injury changed him. Rick's injury made him a stronger person. Rick would not trade his life in a wheelchair for the use of his legs. Rick's courage and dreams make the world a better place.

Glossary

banner: a large sign or piece of cloth with a picture, design, or some writing.

spunk: courage, spirit, energy.

vertebra: a bone in the spinal column.

will: a firm wish or desire.

Talking About the Book

What did you learn about Rick Hansen?

What words would you use to describe Rick?

What challenges has Rick faced in his life?

Describe Rick's act of courage.

Rick sees a banner at the end of the tour. It reads, THE END IS JUST THE BEGINNING. What do you think this means?

Picture Credits